COMETS AND METEOR SHOWERS

A TRUE BOOK

by

Paul P. Sipiera

Children's Press®
A Division of Grolier Publishing

New York London Hong Kong Sydney
Danbury, Connecticut

Comet Halley,
photographed from
Australia in 1986

Reading Consultant
Linda Cornwell
Learning Resource Consultant
Indiana Department of
Education

Science Consultant
Samuel Storch
Lecturer,
American Museum-Hayden
Planetarium, New York City

Dedicated to my friend
Herbert Windolf,
a student of nature

Library of Congress Cataloging-in-Publication Data

Sipiera, Paul P.
    Comets and Meteor Showers / by Paul Sipiera.
    p.   cm. — (A true book)
    Includes bibliographical references and index.
    Summary: Provides an introduction to comets, covering where they
come from, how they travel, their importance to astronomers, as well
as their relationship to meteor showers.
    ISBN 0-516-20330-4 (lib. bdg.)   0-516-26166-5 (pbk.)
    1. Comets—Juvenile literature. 2. Meteorites—Juvenile literature.
[1. Comets. 2. Meteors.] I. Title.   II. Series.
QB721.5.S56 1997
523.6—dc20   96-31711
                                                                         CIP
                                                                          AC

Contents

The Night Sky 5

What Is a Comet? 7

Where Do Comets Come From? 16

Light Shows in the Sky 23

Why Are Comets Important? 29

Did a Comet Kill the Dinosaurs? 31

Are Comets Bad Luck? 35

How to Find a Comet 37

To Find Out More 44

Important Words 46

Index 47

Meet the Author 48

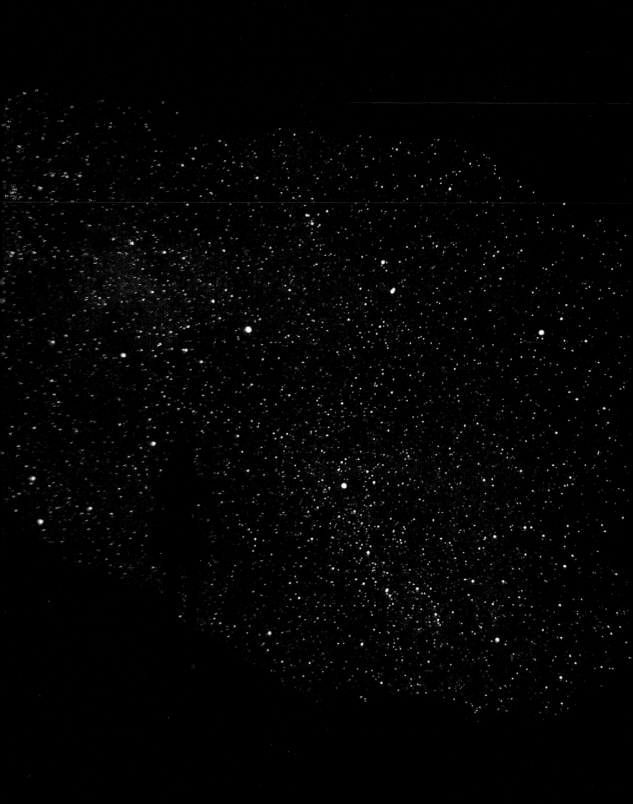

The Night Sky

For thousands of years, people have looked up into the night sky and wondered about the stars. Ancient people made patterns from the brightest stars and called them constellations. These stars seemed to remain the same from year to year.

5

Against this background of stars moved five bright objects. These became known as the planets.

People learned to use the stars to tell time and to predict the seasons. Knowledge of the night sky became important in many cultures.

What Is a Comet?

Every now and then, a new object was seen in the night sky. It was neither a star nor a planet. What was it? Many people saw it as a "hairy star" because of its fuzzy appearance and long tail. Today, we call these objects comets.

This is Comet Halley (above), as seen from Peru in 1910. At first, a comet may appear as only a fuzzy spot in the sky (right).

A comet is a chunk of ice and rock that orbits the Sun. It spends most of its life far from the Sun, where the temperatures are very cold.

Comets are very small, usually about 10 miles

(16 kilometers) across. When a comet is very far from the Sun, it cannot be seen from Earth. But when a comet's orbit brings it close to the Sun, a large cloud of gas forms around it. It is at this point that astronomers can usually first see it.

The central core of a comet, called the nucleus, is small, solid, and made of ice and bits of rock. The comet usually remains solid until it nears the orbit of Uranus, where the Sun's

heat causes the ice to evaporate. This evaporation forms a gas cloud, called a coma, around the nucleus. At this point, the comet can be seen through the largest telescopes.

As the comet gets closer to the Sun, more and more ice evaporates. The coma becomes bigger and brighter.

As a comet comes closer to the hot sun, its ice begins to evaporate, forming a gas cloud called a coma.

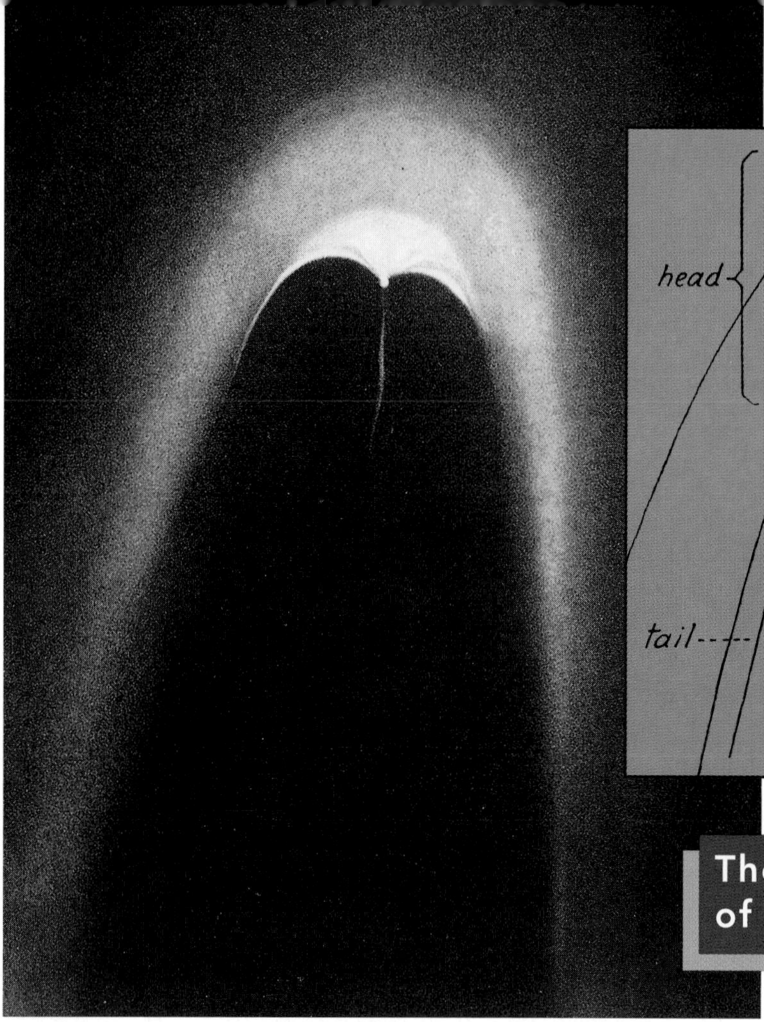

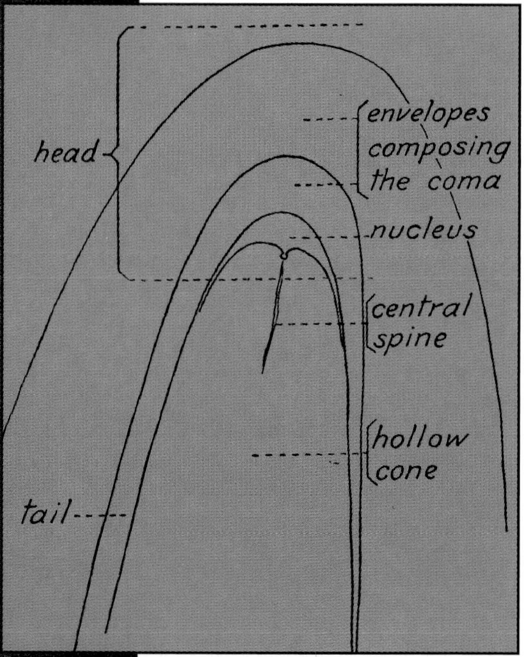
head
envelopes composing the coma
nucleus
central spine
hollow cone
tail

The parts of a comet

By the time the comet reaches the orbit of Mars, a small tail may develop. The tail is formed when powerful solar wind blows gas away from the coma. The tail grows as the comet approaches Earth's orbit. Now, if they know where to look, people can see the comet with binoculars.

At about the time when the comet is as close to the Sun as Earth is, it may actually have two tails. One tail is straight and looks bluish-white. The second tail is curved and has a yellowish color. The bluish-white tail is made of glowing

As it gets closer to the Sun, a comet develops two tails.

gas blown away from the coma. It is always straight and points away from the Sun.

The yellowish curved tail is made of small grains of rock and metal. It is yellow because it reflects the Sun's yellow light. Its curved shape is caused by the motion of the comet as it swings around the Sun. The solar wind does not blow this material away as it does the gas. As these particles melt out of the nucleus, they follow behind the comet like people in a parade.

In this photo of a comet, you can see both the straight, bluish tail and the curved, yellowish tail.

Where Do Comets Come From?

Comets come from a distant part of the solar system called the Oort Cloud. Here, millions of comets slowly orbit the Sun. Sometimes, two comets collide with one another and one is bumped toward the Sun. Sometimes, the gravity of a

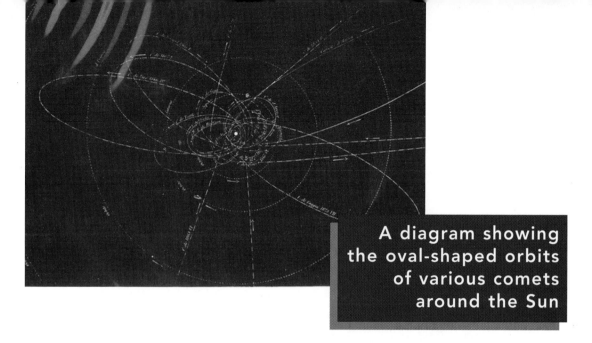

nearby star pulls a comet out of its orbit around the Sun. In turn, the Sun may pull comets away from other stars.

Most comets follow an oval-shaped path around the Sun called an ellipse. Some comets take thousands of years to complete one orbit. Comet

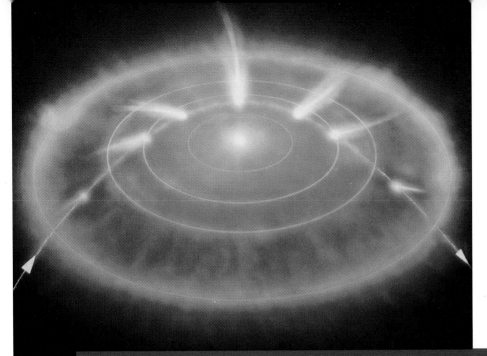

In this drawing, one comet is show in seven different positions of its orbit. The length and direction of the tail changes as the comet travels around the Sun and is shaped by solar wind.

Halley has one of the shorter orbits. It takes about 75 years to travel around the Sun—the average person's lifetime. Author Mark Twain was born in 1835, when Comet Halley was near Earth. In 1910, when it returned, Twain died. He had always said that he came in with the comet and that he would go out with it, too!

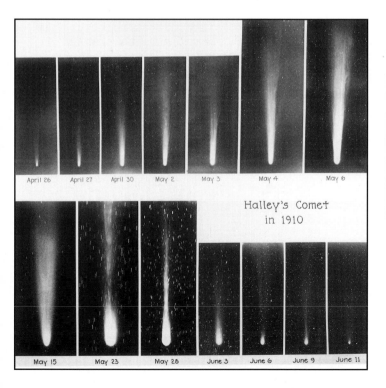

Halley's Comet in 1910

April 26 · April 27 · April 30 · May 2 · May 3 · May 4 · May 6

May 15 · May 23 · May 28 · June 3 · June 6 · June 9 · June 11

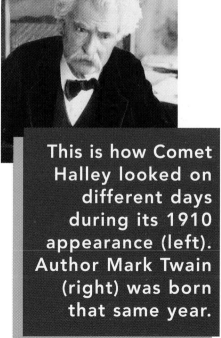

This is how Comet Halley looked on different days during its 1910 appearance (left). Author Mark Twain (right) was born that same year.

Comet Halley

Comet Halley was the first comet shown to have an orbit. In 1705, English astronomer Edmond Halley showed that comets seen in 1531, 1607, and 1682 were really one comet. He predicted that this comet would continue to reappear about every 75 years. The comet was later named after him. Today, new comets are named after whoever discovers them!

Some comets take only a few years to orbit the Sun. Other comets have orbits that bring them close to the Sun once in a 100,000 years, and still others may come only once and never return. It is fun to see the same comet at different times in your life. Seeing it several years apart may bring back good memories.

Unlike the stars and the motion of the planets, comets can be unpredictable.

Sometimes they show up a little earlier—or later—than expected. This depends partly on how close a comet gets to one of the planets. The planet's gravity may pull the comet into a new orbit. The new orbit may be either shorter or longer depending on how great the effect of the gravity. The gas and other material evaporating from the comet can also change its path through space.

Light Shows in the Sky

As a comet passes through the solar system, it leaves behind a trail of dust and rock. Long after a comet has passed, its trail remains in orbit around the Sun. When Earth runs into these old comet trails, the result is a light show in the night sky.

A meteor, also called a "falling star"

A meteor is a small piece of rock or metal that enters the Earth's atmosphere at high speeds and burns up. It is often called a "shooting" or "falling" star. When a number of meteors come from the same direction in the sky, we

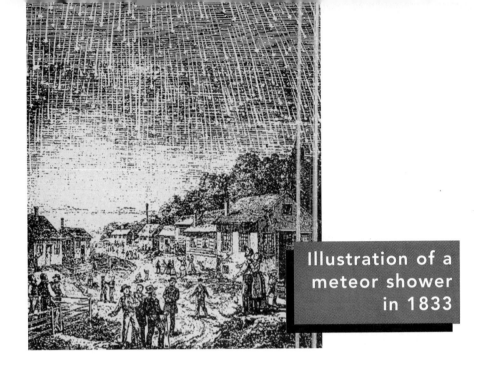

Illustration of a
meteor shower
in 1833

call it a meteor shower. When
a very large number of meteors appear together, we call it
a meteor storm.

Meteor showers and
storms are named for the constellations they seem to be
near. One of the best-known

A Perseid meteor over a campsite in California

showers is the Perseids. These meteors appear to come from the direction of the constellation Perseus on the night of August 11. On a clear, moonless night away from bright city lights, a person may see more than 60 meteors per hour. They appear as fast but rather faint streaks of light.

Meteor storms are less frequent, but last longer and look brighter. This is true of the Leonids, from the direction

A false-color photograph of a Leonid meteor shower

of Leo. The Leonid storm can be seen once every 33 years. At the height of the storm, there may be more than 100,000 meteors per hour. This happens because Earth passes through a very dense region of the dust trail. These meteors light up the sky all night long. The next Leonid meteor storm will occur on the night of November 17, 1999. After that, you'll have to wait till 2032!

Why Are Comets Important?

Comets are believed to be the leftover material from the formation of the solar system. They may be more than 4.6 billion years old.

Some scientists believe that comets may have brought the chemical compounds that first

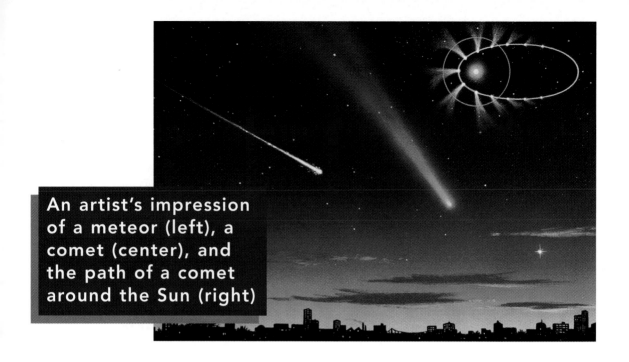

An artist's impression of a meteor (left), a comet (center), and the path of a comet around the Sun (right)

formed life on Earth. Comets contain water and certain chemicals that life depends on. One day soon, scientists will send a spacecraft to a comet to sample it. Then we will have a better idea of how comets may have contributed to life on Earth.

Did a Comet Kill the Dinosaurs?

Just as comets may have brought life to Earth, they may also have brought death. Many scientists believe that a large comet caused the extinction of the dinosaurs.

Every now and then, a comet hits Earth. When this happens, Earth's climate can change and many different life forms may die.

An artist's impression of dinosaurs being startled by a huge comet heading toward Earth

About 65 million years ago, all the dinosaurs died. For more than 150 million years before that, dinosaurs had populated Earth. Many grew to an enormous size, and some were able to fly. Then, they suddenly disappeared. Many scientists believe that a giant comet or a small asteroid struck Earth. A large crater formed, and dust was thrown high into the atmosphere. This may have blocked out sunlight and darkened the skies for several years, producing what is called a "global winter."

Many scientists believe that the dinosaurs died out because of a "global winter" caused by a giant comet hitting Earth. This would have thrown dust high into the air, blocking out the sun's light and heat for perhaps several years.

Many dinosaurs died from the effects of the blast. Those that survived slowly starved to death. Most dinosaurs were plant-eaters. Without sunlight, most plants died out, and there was no food for the dinosaurs. By the time the skies cleared, the dinosaurs were all gone.

Are Comets Bad Luck?

Today, most people do not fear comets—they look forward to seeing them. But that has not always been true. In the past, some people thought comets brought bad luck. Whenever anything really bad happened, there seemed to be a comet in the sky. When a terrible sickness killed thousands of people, or

when a city was destroyed by fire, there was a comet to blame.

Today, we know that the comets we see in the sky have no effect on what happens on Earth. People long ago had to blame disasters on something, and a comet sometimes just happened to be there.

How to Find a Comet

Most comets are discovered by accident. An astronomer may be taking photographs of stars when a new comet happens to appear in the sky. However, some astronomers conduct comet hunts. They search the sky night after night, looking for a fuzzy spot

that moves. Once a comet has been seen, no one is sure if it will become big and bright, or remain just a faint object in the telescope.

The brightness of a comet is hard to predict. Some comets that astronomers think will be spectacular fizzle out and never

get bright. Others provide
pleasant surprises. In 1976, a
comet named West was just
average at best before it passed
around the Sun. As it came
around, it broke into five pieces.
This produced a beautiful tail
that was very easy to see.

Comet West, which
last appeared in 1976

In 1995, a comet named
Hale-Bopp was discovered at
a point very far from the Sun.
Since it was seen from such a
great distance, it was predicted to be very bright when it
passed Earth in April 1997. In
January 1996, as astronomers

waited for Hale-Bopp, an unexpected bright comet was discovered—Comet Hyakutake. It was a beautiful sight in the evening sky for

Comet Hyakutake

more than two months. Many people got their first look at a comet at this time.

A great number of comets are discovered by amateur astronomers. If you are lucky enough to find one, it will be named after you. Someday, you might become very interested in astronomy and search for comets. If you succeed, your name will be among the stars.

An illustration of children viewing
a comet in the night sky

43

To Find Out More

Here are some additional resources to help you learn more about comets and meteor showers:

 **Books**

 **Organizations**

Burrows, William E,. **Mission to Deep Space: Voyagers' Journey of Discovery.** W.H. Freeman and Company, 1993.

Curtis, Anthony R., ed., **Space Almanac.** Gulf Publishing Company, 1992.

Van Cleave, Janice, **Astronomy for Every Kid: 101 Easy Experiments that Really Work.** John Wiley & Sons, 1991.

Astronomical Society of the Pacific
1290 24th Avenue
San Francisco, CA 94122
http://www.physics.sfsu.edu /asp

Junior Astronomical Society
58 Vaughan Gardens
Ilford Essex IG1 3PD
England

The Planetary Society
5 North Catalina Avenue
Pasadena, CA 91106
e-mail: *tps.lc@genie.geis. com*

Online Sites

Astronomy Online!
http://www.eaglequest.com /%7Eastro/

Comets and Meteor Showers
http://medinfo.wustl.edu /%7Ekronkg/index.html

Comet Hale-Bopp Online
www.halebopp.com

Comet Hyakutake Information
http://www.sji.org/ed/ hyakinfo.html

Sky and Telescope's Comet Page
http:/www.skypub.com/ comets/comets.html

The Comet Watch Program - Last Night's Comets
http://www.mindspring.com /%7Etpuckett/comets.html

Important Words

atmosphere the gases that surround a planet; the air

asteroid small planetlike object that orbits the Sun between Mars and Jupiter

coma large gas cloud that surrounds the solid part of a comet

ellipse oval or egg-shaped path or orbit

extinction when all members of a certain kind of plant or animal die out

evaporate when a solid or liquid turns into a gas from being heated

gravity the force of attraction between two objects

solar wind gaslike substance constantly being thrown off by the Sun into space

Index

(**Boldface** page numbers
   indicate illustrations.)

asteroid, 33
astronomer, 9, 20, 37, 42
atmosphere, 24, 33
coma, 10, 11, **11, 12,** 13,
   14
Comet Hale-Bopp, 40,
   40
Comet Halley, **2, 8,** 18,
   19, **19,** 20, **21**
Comet Hyakutake, 41-
   42, **41**
Comet West, 39
constellation, 5, 25, 26
crater, 33
dinosaurs, 31, 32-34, **32,
   34**
disasters, 35-36
dust, 23, 33
Earth, 9,13,19, 23, 24,
   28,30, 31, 33-34, 36
extinction, 31
gas, 9, 10, 13, 14, 15, 22
global winter, 33, **34**

gravity, 16-17, 22
Hale-Bopp, 40-42
Halley, Edmond, 20, **20**
ice, 8, 9, 10, 11
Leonids, 27-28, **27**
Mars, 12
meteor, 24, **24, 30**
meteor shower, 23-28, **25**
meteor storm, 25, 27-28
night sky, 5, 6, 7
nucleus, 9, 10, **10, 12**
Oort Cloud, 16
orbit of comets, 8, 9, 16-
   18, **17, 18,** 20, 21-22,
   23
Perseids, 25-26, **26**
Perseus, 26
solar system, 16, 23, 29
solar wind, 12-13, 15, **18**
star, 5, 6, 7, 17, 21, 37
Sun, 8, 9, 10, 11, 13, 14,
   15, 16, 17, 18, 21, 23,
   33, 34, 40
tails, 12, 13, 14, **14, 15**
Twain, Mark, 19, **19**
Uranus, 9

Meet the Author

Paul P. Sipiera is a professor of geology and astronomy at William Rainey Harper College in Palatine, Illinois. His main area of research is meteorites. When he is not studying science, he can be found working on his farm in Galena, Illinois, with his wife, Diane, and their three daughters, Andrea, Paula Frances, and Carrie Ann.